IMAGES
of America

THE 1972 BLACK HILLS FLOOD

IMAGES
of America

THE 1972 BLACK HILLS FLOOD

Corey Christianson

ARCADIA
PUBLISHING

Published by Arcadia Publishing
Charleston, South Carolina

Printed in the United States of America

Library of Congress Control Number: 2023950810

For all general information, please contact Arcadia Publishing:
Telephone 843-853-2070
Fax 843-853-0044
E-mail sales@arcadiapublishing.com

Visit us on the Internet at www.arcadiapublishing.com

*This book is dedicated to all who died during the 1972
Black Hills flood—you will never be forgotten.*

CONTENTS

ACKNOWLEDGMENTS

The 1972 Black Hills flood occurred 52 years ago at the time of publication of this book. The number of images, histories, and memories that exist within the Black Hills are innumerable. It is my hope that this book sheds some light on the disaster and the recovery that occurred in the Black Hills in 1972.

There are multiple organizations that helped me with the gathering of images and gave me insight into the disaster over the years of research: I want to thank the Rapid City Public Library, as well as Sam Slocum and Krista Licht, for helping me gather and scan images. I could not have done this book without their willingness to help me from over 100 miles away.

Thank you to the US Air Force (USAF), Ellsworth Air Force Base, and especially base historian John Moyes. Ellsworth Air Force Base was an integral part of the recovery of the 1972 Black Hills flood, and to be able to tell the story with the images from the USAF is wonderful. The South Dakota National Guard needs a thank-you as well—its efforts matched Ellsworth Air Force Base's during the flood. Accessing and sharing the images is an honor and allows the story of the 1972 Black Hills flood to be told in a more complete way. Thank you, as well, to the Rapid City Police Department for being willing to share its history.

Thank you to the Keystone Area Historical Society and Casey Sullivan. The images gathered from the Keystone Area Historical Society help tell a more complete story encompassing all of the Black Hills. I am always grateful, Casey, that you were an intern for me and that we changed our focus on the 1972 Black Hills flood thanks to your internship.

Thank you to Simpson's Printing, a business that survived the flood, for supporting the projects that we did over the years and for the beautiful map that is in this book.

I need to thank both sides of my family, and my friends, who maybe didn't understand my enthusiasm with this research but always supported me; Dr. Kurt Hackemer, who prodded me along and told me some of the best advice for writing a book; and my editor, Amy Jarvis, for being so flexible and able to answer any of my questions.

Of course, to my husband, Mac, thank you for editing the roughest drafts, listening to my rants, asking questions, and generally supporting me through the years. I couldn't have done any of this without you, and I love you.

INTRODUCTION

South Dakota, as with any state in North America, has a varied and unique history that extends beyond the date of its statehood. An area within the state with a particularly abundant history is the beautiful Black Hills, which are nestled on the western border of South Dakota and stretch into Wyoming. Long before the time of settlers, the Black Hills were considered a sacred place for the Native American populations that lived around the country. Creation stories for the Plains Indians stem from the Black Hills, specifically at Wind Cave National Monument. Even today, the Black Hills are honored and revered, many of the monuments that can be found in the Black Hills have prayer bundles secured to trees, and other cultural ceremonies are held at the monuments.

While still a sacred land for Native Americans, the Black Hills have expanded into an attraction to persons around the globe who come to see the vast rolling hills covered in Black Hills pine trees, as well as the monuments erected to celebrate Founding Fathers and other American leaders at Mount Rushmore, or the brave Lakota warrior Crazy Horse, forever honored in his own monument. These attractions, and the Black Hills they call home, draw millions of visitors a year and have for more than a century. These attractions have caused tourism to become the second-largest industry in South Dakota after agriculture.

Along with a vast history and oceans of pines, the Black Hills are known for their own unique weather patterns—specifically, weather unique from the remainder of the state. Lead, South Dakota, is a town nestled in the hills known for snowfall early into the autumn, perhaps even at the end of September. The area is known for hail storms, which seemingly appear at random and last for a few minutes before disappearing. Rapid City is especially susceptible to flooding, and there have been floods both large and small over the decades of the city's existence. Some of these floods caused minor damage—flooding in basements, some wet lawns—and some of the floods over the years took lives.

June 9, 1972, was a day that started with heavy clouds hanging over the Black Hills. Survivors of the oncoming disaster remember the clouds having a greenish tinge, an ominous color for the sky. The forecasts for the day reported that there were going to be thunderstorms, an understatement that haunts the Black Hills to this day. In the afternoon and evening of June 9, the thunderstorms and subsequent heavy rains that followed caused an increase in the volume of water running through the creeks in the northern Black Hills. The creeks were so overwhelmed with water that dam failures in the northern Black Hills occurred, which caused more volumes of water to come into Rapid Creek in a tragic domino effect that cost many their lives.

Rapid Creek runs through the center of Rapid City; Rapid City itself is in the foothills of the Black Hills. By the time the floodwater from the northern Black Hills hit Canyon Lake Dam in Rapid City, it was full of debris from the Black Hills creek systems. Canyon Lake Dam, on the western side of Rapid City, failed due to the debris and overwhelming water. When Canyon Lake Dam failed, the increase of water and debris that traveled through Rapid City Creek caused more damage than any flood ever had before. The chaos that followed was all-encompassing. In modern numbers, there was over $1 billion worth of damage—the damage to businesses, cars, and roads in the Black Hills was incredibly devastating.

The night of June 9 was summed up in one sentence in the *Rapid City Journal* later in June: "It's rather like war, isn't it?" To the survivors, the night of the flood was like war. There was a loss of electricity, the roar of rushing water, and the cries and screams for help and of fear. Helicopters and boats were heard intermittently trying to rescue those who couldn't get away from the rising water fast enough. Men, women, and children, old and young—they were all affected by the rising water and the fear.

The flood lasted for less than 12 hours. By 5:00 a.m. on June 10, the water was back within its banks in the creeks of the Black Hills. June 10 presented its own issues: the lack of electricity, and all utilities, meant that there was no potable water for survivors of the disaster. The buildup of debris in the towns in the Black Hills caused movement issues for recovery processes, especially because when the flooding water moved through the hills it did damage to the roads and the bridges that connect towns.

There was also a problem regarding the survivors and fatalities of the flood. People were missing, and there were bodies that littered the flooded area, fatalities that could not get away from the water in time. The bodies needed to be recovered, identified, and buried; those who were missing needed to be identified and, hopefully, found. A group of individuals, led by World War II veteran and sheriff's office deputy Chuck Childs, spent months after the flooding searching and recovering missing persons, getting the list from over 10,000 to only 5 missing people by November 1972. Burials were held en masse; the final count, including the 5 missing and presumed dead, would be over 200—this number comes from all the Black Hills, not just Rapid City.

The rescue and recovery of the Black Hills would not have occurred without the South Dakota National Guard, Ellsworth Air Force Base, local law enforcement and fire departments, the civilians who call the Black Hills home, and the tourists who were visiting at the time. The community came together during and after the flood for recovery processes that made national news, and the United States responded with monetary and material donations that allowed the survivors of the disaster to focus on recovery without having to worry about basic needs. Donations and letters of support from countries like Japan and Brazil lifted the spirits of South Dakotans.

In the immediate aftermath of the flood, the first application for emergency housing was accepted at 1:00 p.m. on June 10, just hours after the flood was deemed "over." The Department of Housing and Urban Development (HUD) office in Rapid City and the response of the personnel was one of the first signs of hope after the disaster. The mobile homes brought in from HUD did have their own issues, even though they were useful in housing displaced families. Issues in the units included the mixing of people from different social and economic backgrounds and financial issues, with the homes sometimes being more costly than what the previous housing cost for families. The goal of these temporary homes was simple: to give displaced residents from Rapid City a place to live in the short term. HUD officials expected that most families would find permanent housing within a year after the flood.

Housing opportunities were not equal for all citizens of Rapid City. The Native American population of Rapid City, many of whom lost their homes during the flood due to living right on Rapid Creek in Camp Oshkosh, did not have the same opportunities for housing as other citizens did in the aftermath of the flood. They were pushed off into a section of Rapid City called the "Sioux Addition," which still exists to this day. Other individuals decided to leave the Black Hills after the flooding, never to return—it was too hard to stay where a tragedy had occurred, or it was too hard to completely start over in the aftermath of the flooding.

The other areas of the Black Hills had less support from HUD, not for any reason but because it was less needed. While people did utilize HUD for temporary housing, many of the communities were more affected by the loss of campgrounds and cabins, which HUD did not necessarily cover.

The US Congress passed the Flood Disaster Protection Act of 1973 after the 1972 Black Hills Flood. This act requires that flood insurance protection be purchased for any project located in specific areas designated as 100-year or 500-year floodplains. The act was designed to minimize future flooding issues and help individuals recover after flooding.

The Black Hills haven't completely changed since the flood, but there have been some landscaping changes that have occurred due to the water. This is especially noticeable in Rapid City, which focused on not allowing anyone in the flood plain after so many people died. Today, no one is allowed to live in the floodplain around Rapid Creek, though businesses are located around the creek. Instead, there are hundreds of acres of parks, golf courses, and bike paths along Rapid Creek; there are also signs along the creek that talk about the chaos and destruction of the flooding. There are multiple memorials set up in the Black Hills highlighting all the fatalities of the flooding as well.

These greenspaces came about thanks to the efforts of Leonard Swanson, as well as the Rapid City City Council. Leonard Swanson, who was elected director of the Rapid City Urban Renewal Program in the aftermath of the 1972 Black Hills flood, teared up in a meeting with the city council when they were discussing housing options for those who had been displaced by the flood. He recognized that living next to the creek caused much of the death and destruction and that the city had to develop a plan to mitigate potential future disasters. Today, there are regulations that dictate what insurance people need to have to live on or near a floodplain.

The Federal Emergency Management Agency, also known as FEMA, was established on April 1, 1979, shortly after the partial meltdown of Three Mile Island Nuclear Generating Station in Pennsylvania. The goal of FEMA was to have a coordinated, organized response to any emergency and allow for a consolidated emergency preparedness plan. FEMA utilizes response from the military, local first responders, and other organizations to make sure that disaster response is done with the most lives saved as possible, very similar to the actions of responders during the Black Hills flood.

In 1998, twenty-six years after the flooding that did huge amounts of damage to the Black Hills, FEMA identified areas in Rapid City that could be, and now are, considered special flood hazard areas and therefore fall under the Flood Disaster Protection Act. What this means, though, is that for 26 years, there was no official application of the Flood Disaster Protection Act in Rapid City or the Black Hills area. It was a stroke of luck that there were no other floods in that time.

Every year on the commemoration of the 1972 Black Hills flood, there is some sort of remembrance held in the Black Hills. In 2022, the 50th commemoration, there was a week-long remembrance of the flood and a celebration of the recovery from the flooding. However, some people still don't want to talk about the flooding. The tragedy affected everyone, but everyone experienced it differently, and there is a percentage of citizens in the Black Hills who choose to ignore the disaster that occurred rather than remember it. This makes gathering the history of the tragedy difficult if not downright impossible. But forgetting the tragedy is not a possibility either—to forget means that the tragedy could be repeated, and that is not going to be an option in the future. The Black Hills have better emergency protocols in place today if there is another flood event.

There are devices that measure the speed of the water coming through creeks in the Black Hills, and weather forecasts are more accurate. There are also two military bases in the Black Hills, the same that responded to the flooding in 1972. Every year, the South Dakota National Guard puts on training with other military entities in the Black Hills to practice not only emergency response but also military actions. With the multiple, up-to-date emergency management protocols in place, there is less of a chance that there will ever be a flood event to this extent again.

This book is not going to cover one main aspect of the flooding: the fatalities. While it is important to recognize that there were fatalities during the flood, the families of those lost during the flood get overwhelmed every year with memories and images of their loved ones that were lost. Over 200 lives were lost in the flood, 17 of whom were military and first responders. Included in this number are also the 5 missing individuals. There was another flood within the week after the flood of June 9. Sadly, 2 more lives were lost that night, and they count in the fatality list from June 9 as well. This book is going to focus on the disaster itself, along with the recovery process. Images of damaged homes and businesses, soldiers and airmen, and landscapes are the images found in this book. Images of fatalities can be found at the Rapid City Public Library.

The past 50 years have proven to be a time of growth for the Black Hills, but the 1972 Black Hills flood needs to be remembered for continued success and recovery.

The appearance of South Dakota National Guard (SDNG) and/or US Department of Defense (DoD) visual information does not imply or constitute SDNG/DoD endorsement.

One

THE BLACK HILLS AND THE FLOOD

South Dakota is a state of beautiful landscapes. As a visitor crosses the Missouri River and continues to drive westward, they are greeted by the rising rock formations of Badlands National Park. The Badlands are a huge part of South Dakota tourism, something that was directly affected by the Black Hills flood in 1972. (Courtesy of the Rapid City Public Library.)

The formations in Badlands National Park, much like the formations in the Black Hills, were formed by an inland sea that existed millions of years ago. They are continually affected by weather experiences that cause erosion. These formations are home to prehistoric history, Native American history, settler history, and military history as well. They also house a huge amount of geological information within the layers; though this image does not show it, there are layers of red, orange, yellow, tan, and more colors of rock that indicate what the timeline of growth was that these formations went through. These formations signal the entrance to the Black Hills and are visible on clear days from Black Elk Peak. The Black Hills are similar in that they are affected by weather patterns and creeks that run through the area and have an immense and varied history. (Courtesy of the Rapid City Public Library.)

The Black Hills are considered sacred by many Native American tribes in the United States. They are also a huge tourism asset to the state of South Dakota, with the well-known Mount Rushmore calling the Black Hills home. Mount Rushmore is well known as the "Shrine of Democracy," a monument that emphasizes what the United States is. Mount Rushmore was completed long before the 1972 Black Hills flood and had already made itself known by 1972 as a major tourist attraction; what had not been realized yet, but soon would be, is the fact that because Mount Rushmore is in such a great position in the Black Hills, it would be a great spot for people to take shelter from a flooding disaster. Individuals from Keystone ended up taking shelter at Mount Rushmore on the night of June 9, 1972. (Courtesy of the Rapid City Public Library.)

The tourism industry made this flooding disaster even more horrific. The tourism industry in the Black Hills relies on visitors camping near, traveling to, and staying in the local communities to visit the monuments and other activities that exist in the Black Hills. When the flooding on June 9 occurred, there was a very real threat to tourists in the area, especially to those who were camping. Directly after the flooding, it was declared that the Black Hills would stay open for tourists, with directions for visitors to move around the area by using indirect means and avoiding Rapid City and Keystone, among other areas. This was done so that the income for the area would not decrease too much. But for the tourists already in those areas, their vacations took a turn toward difficult—and potentially deadly. (Courtesy of the Rapid City Public Library.)

Ellsworth Air Force Base opened in 1942 as Rapid City Army Air Base. Having gone through multiple name changes over the years does not mean that Ellsworth Air Force Base ever disappeared; in the decades that followed the opening of the base, citizens of the Black Hills embraced the airmen as locals. The base has played an important role in military response to world affairs since World War II. From being a training base for bombers to being a base that housed missileers to being a home for modern-day bombers and a future training base, Ellsworth Air Force Base has been a staple in Black Hills history. The men who were stationed at Ellsworth Air Force Base on the day of June 9, 1972, would end up playing a huge part in the recovery process. (Courtesy of the Rapid City Public Library.)

A unique opportunity was taken on the morning of the 1972 Black Hills flood. The Rapid City Police Department, including officers and administrative staff, posed outside of the police department for a group image. Most of the men in uniform in this image ended up serving that evening, some spending over 24 hours actively working for the disaster response and recovery. In his investigation report, Lt. Thomas Hennies praised the work of the police department in the recovery processes. He went on to highlight the items that could be added to the cars the Rapid City Police Department would use in response to another disaster like the flood. The police station in the background ended up having the lower floors, as well as the parking lot nearby, completely flooded by the rising waters. Today, the building is a shelter, still located along Rapid Creek. (Courtesy of the Rapid City Police Department.)

Images of the chaos of the flood, the high water, and the active destruction and devastation are rare. This image exemplifies why—the water on the night of the flood overwhelmed the banks of all the creeks that it moved through. In Rapid City, the water reached a height of 15 feet, 9 inches. It was an extremely quick flood as well, lasting less than 12 hours but doing more damage than any flood in South Dakota at that point in time. Taking photographs of the flooding while it was occurring was dangerous but necessary so that after-action reports could be completed with accuracy. This image was most likely taken in the early morning hours of June 10, as the sun was rising and the first light was coming through the clouds. Taken from a bridge, the damage that the water had caused is easily visible in the background of this photograph. (Courtesy of the South Dakota National Guard.)

As soon as the sun rose on June 10, a couple of major problems in Rapid City were realized. While Rapid Creek had gotten back within its banks by 5:00 a.m., it left behind huge patches of standing water. This posed a huge problem in the recovery process: if there were electrical wires in standing water, they could be electrified without people realizing it. The other issue that stems from standing water is that there are multiple diseases that could be passed and grow quite easily. Getting rid of the standing water was a priority in the recovery process because of the threat that it posed to the communities that had survived the original flooding. (Both, courtesy of the Rapid City Public Library.)

The damage to the natural growth around the creeks of the Black Hills is not often considered but should be. With all the debris that came down from the Black Hills, it is amazing that the damage was not worse. Coming from the northern Black Hills, trees were taken out and completely knocked over, especially if they were right next to the creek system; roots were upturned and damaged beyond recovery. Much of the clean-up was spent digging out trees and plants that were beyond saving. Trees that were completely knocked over were often pushed by the floodwaters as one piece and would not be broken unless they came up against something, like a bridge or a foundation for a house. Because of this, many of the trees ended up causing more damage to the areas surrounding the flooded creeks. (Courtesy of the Rapid City Public Library.)

During the night of the flood on June 9, at about midnight, two men of the 109th Engineering Group, part of the South Dakota National Guard, moved two five-gallon gas cans each across the top of the dam pictured to fuel the pumps, hopefully protecting the dam against the floodwaters. They were struggling to keep up with the flooding waters all night without fuel. Here, they are inspecting the dam for damage after the flooding; many dams failed due to overwhelming water and debris. Damage can be seen on the far side of the image; the writing on the dam reads "cut on the dotted line." By all accounts, having to fuel the dam was a very terrifying experience for the two men. (Courtesy of the South Dakota National Guard.)

Two

RECOVERY IN RAPID CITY

The damage from the 1972 Black Hills flood was all-encompassing. With power lines down, a lack of access to clean water, water damage, debris damage, threats of illness, lack of food, and more, the citizens of Rapid City and the Black Hills were stuck questioning what would happen to them next. (Courtesy of the Rapid City Public Library.)

Ellsworth Air Force Base and the South Dakota National Guard became an incredibly important part of the recovery process. Emergency canteens from other Air Force bases were sent to Ellsworth to aid the recovery process; Ellsworth Air Force Base ended up welcoming canteens, search and rescue crews, and supply drops from all over the nation. Ellsworth Air Force Base and the South Dakota National Guard base also opened their doors to the communities in the Black Hills. They hosted displaced persons, gave out thousands of inoculations, issued meals and clean water, and gave out donations. Beyond all of this, the men involved at both Ellsworth Air Force Base and the South Dakota National Guard spent days at a time awake, helping with the recovery processes however they could. (Above, courtesy of the US Air Force; below, courtesy of the South Dakota National Guard.)

Immediately, the priorities for recovery from the 1972 Black Hills flood were two-fold: search and rescue and clean-up. Volunteers from all over the nation filtered into Rapid City and the surrounding areas to help with the clean-up process; at one point, volunteers were being turned away because there was not enough work to keep everyone busy. Working dog teams from Wyoming and Colorado made their way to the Black Hills to help with fatality recovery as well as search and rescue; federal agents, including deputies from the US Marshal Service, aided both the law enforcement of the Black Hills and the recovery aspects. Religious groups, national organizations, and government officials all wanted to help the recovery in some way. (Courtesy of the Rapid City Public Library.)

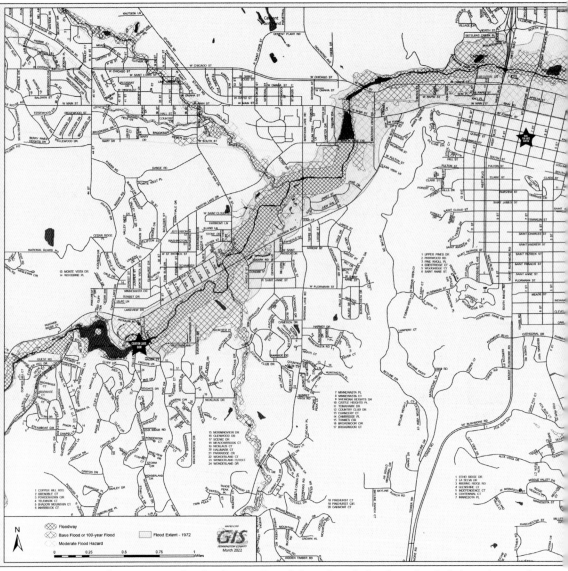

This map demonstrates the flooding in Rapid City. Rapid Creek is the dark line that snakes through the map, with the shaded areas showing where the water had overtopped its banks and where the water wiped out neighborhoods, businesses, railroad tracks, and the small parks that existed in Rapid City at the time. The stars indicate the Dahl Fine Arts Center, the Journey

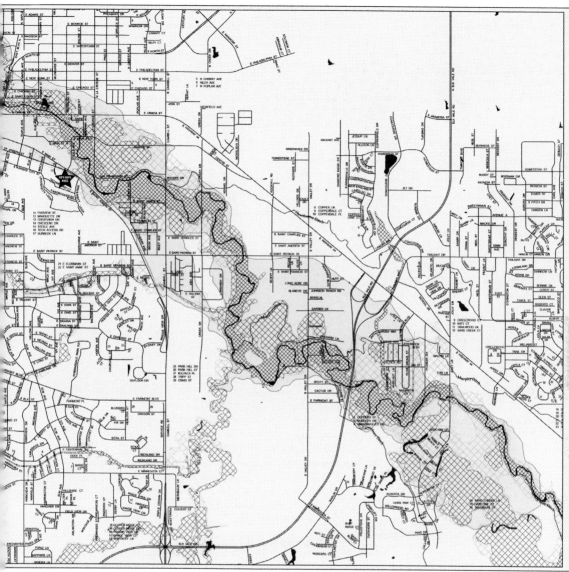

Museum and Learning Center, Canyon Lake Dam, and the South Dakota School of Mines and Technology. This map, based on historical maps and descriptions, was created for the award-winning 1972 Black Hills Flood Commemoration Exhibit, put on by the Journey Museum and Learning Center in Rapid City. (Courtesy of Simpson's Printing.)

Rapid City faced a huge issue in the aftermath of the flooding in the shape of the buildup of debris. To get rid of the debris piles all around the community, heavy machinery had to be brought in, and specific areas were designated as places to get rid of the debris once it was cleaned up. The debris gathered started higher in the Black Hills as the creeks overflowed their banks. Here, the debris can be seen stuck under a bridge in Rapid City. Also in this image is the heavy equipment that was used to move the debris and clear the bridge so that it could eventually be used again for vehicles. The man on the bridge seems to be overseeing the debris removal process. (Courtesy of the Rapid City Public Library.)

Trees, plants, and dirt were sucked into the creeks, traveling down toward Nemo, Keystone, and Rapid City. But that does not even consider the cars that were moved by the floodwaters as well. This image shows a building in Rapid City whose surrounding area was demolished by the flood. In the foreground sits what looks to be a fence or a roof; in the background, cars stacked on top of each other and a ruined fence indicate the power the floodwaters had. The standing water can be seen in this image as well, another dangerous aspect of the flooding to Rapid City locals due to illness and insects. The building in the very far background has a damaged exterior, including what looks to be a storage door or a garage door completely bent in from the water. (Courtesy of the South Dakota National Guard.)

The floodwaters that came down from the Black Hills caused more damage than anyone had seen from a natural disaster before. When flooding occurred in Nemo, Keystone, Rapid City, and other communities around the Black Hills, more debris fell into the moving water and caused more debris to build up in a never-ending cycle. Railroad tracks loosened from their bases; concrete bridges were either damaged or destroyed. Transportation opportunities were all but halted because of the 1972 Black Hills flood. Here is a very good example of how railroad tracks can be taken off their beds and moved around all because of floodwaters. The erosion of the land under the railroad tracks was one of the top reasons why the tracks moved; the land pictured here is eaten away from the water. (Courtesy of the Rapid City Public Library.)

This undated image of Canyon Lake Dam, located in Rapid City, was taken prior to the 1972 Black Hills flood. The earthen dam in this image was built 40 years before the flood occurred. On the night of June 9, at around 11:00 p.m., this dam failed. Debris from the northern Black Hills and all the dams that had failed previously, plus the homes and campgrounds along the many creeks, barreled into Canyon Lake Dam. First, the debris and water went over the top; then the debris and water went through the dam itself, as it was only an earthen dam. Rebuilding the dam in the aftermath was slow; the Army Corps of Engineers regulated how Canyon Lake would have to be for the new dam to handle the movement of water that would equal, or even exceed, the amount of water that moved through on the night of June 9. (Courtesy of the Black Hills National Forest Historical Collection, Leland D. Case Library for Western Historical Studies, Black Hills State University.)

The damage to the natural growth around the creeks of the Black Hills is not often considered but should be. With all the debris that came down from the Black Hills, trees were taken out and completely knocked over; roots were upturned and damaged beyond recovery. Much of the clean-up was spent digging out trees and plants that were beyond saving. This heavy machinery is doing just that. Much of the heavy machinery was used to move debris, telephone poles, and other items that were too large to shift otherwise. Often, this heavy machinery came from the South Dakota National Guard or Ellsworth Air Force Base, but electrical businesses, agricultural businesses, and others lent their gear for clean-up work as well. Much of the major and dangerous debris was cleaned up by the end of the first week after the flood, at least in Rapid City. (Courtesy of the Rapid City Public Library.)

Perhaps one of the strangest views that community members saw after the flooding was over was the location of vehicles around their towns and cities. Cars can float and move in water with seemingly no organization, and as a result, there were cars that were stacked together in strange ways, pushed up against trees, and upside down in the middle of fields. The image below shows a wrecked automobile, and much more debris, before it was moved. (Both, courtesy of the Rapid City Public Library.)

The power lines in the background of this image highlight an important part of the disaster, especially in Rapid City. The floodwaters, full of debris, caused issues with the electrical grid in Rapid City, causing the city to lose power and water access. Without electricity and clean water access, Rapid City was pushed into a world where communication was difficult, and the safety of the citizens was paramount. The downed power lines also caused more danger for recovery efforts; with downed power lines, the floodwaters became more dangerous for those involved. Locating the downed power lines and getting them out of the way of the recovery processes were the first steps in the effort to get the electricity back up in Rapid City. After that, the effort turned to fixing telephone poles and electrical lines that were damaged in the flooding or installing new ones. (Courtesy of the Rapid City Public Library.)

Electricity was 90 percent restored to Rapid City within a week of the Black Hills flood, but that took around-the-clock effort to get the electricity back up and running by multiple electric companies; many of the men who worked for those companies worked 24-hour days, sometimes longer, without sleep. Once the electricity was back up, recovery processes and communication were made much easier—and worried friends and families outside of the state of South Dakota could contact their families again. Citizens of Rapid City were warned to boil water before using or consuming it because of the threats of malaria, typhoid, and other illnesses. Clean water was being handed out, but it was handed out faster than it could be donated. Efforts to get clean water back up for citizens were a very high priority. (Courtesy of the Rapid City Public Library.)

A lot of the debris that made it to Rapid City was wood from homes that the water wiped out as it came down from the northern Black Hills. This debris, with its sharp edges and the speed with which it moved, caused more damage than the water itself. (Courtesy of the South Dakota National Guard.)

These piles of debris held their own dangers. Warped metal, trapped mud, and debris could cause injury to the responders. The debris piles could also hide fatalities of the flood, though the one pictured here did not. These became some of the most terrifying pieces of the aftermath of the flooding because they were an unknown. (Courtesy of the South Dakota National Guard.)

The cars in the background of this image were not placed here purposely; the floodwaters deposited them here as they receded back into Rapid Creek. This pile of debris, and others, caused issues. Search and rescue and recovery crews had to maneuver themselves around a lot of debris to do their jobs. With the floodwaters came debris, cars, and railroad ties that caused obstacles to be stacked up and deposited away from where they originated. Recovery crews had to move the debris to another space to clear out areas, like this railroad yard, for reuse and rebuilding later. Search and rescue crews especially looked in and around the piles of debris for survivors and fatalities of the flood. Sadly, many of the recovery efforts did find fatalities; this is one of the reasons that survivors do not speak of the flooding tragedy today. (Courtesy of the Rapid City Public Library.)

Another strange view for citizens in the Black Hills was the open ground. When the waters came through, they washed everything downstream. Everything that was not solidly attached—and some things that were—disappeared into the swirling water, leaving behind little glimpses of what the landscape was like before the urbanization of the Black Hills. (Courtesy of the South Dakota National Guard.)

The damage along Rapid Creek was immense as well. Beyond debris from the northern Black Hills and the homes that were along the creek, there was an increase in silt and mud deposits after the floodwaters went back down. The whole of Rapid Creek's shape was warped and changed due to the flood. (Courtesy of the Rapid City Public Library.)

Bridges had been blown out during the flood—not by water, but by the debris that the water carried. The debris seen here was part of the debris that wiped out a bridge in Rapid City. A blown-out bridge caused transportation issues and slowed down the recovery process. (Courtesy of the Rapid City Public Library.)

Immediately, one of the challenges was getting the people who were going to help with the recovery processes where they needed to go. Temporary bridges, and temporary fixes to permanent bridges, were created to pass recovery implements and vehicles from one area of Rapid City to another. (Courtesy of the South Dakota National Guard.)

This is the Ford car dealership in Rapid City after the 1972 Black Hills flood. The business was damaged and most likely became one of the many businesses that was considered a loss after the floodwaters receded. Over 500 businesses in the Black Hills were damaged by the flood. Some of the businesses that were in the flooding waters were used as a place of refuge; some were completely wiped out, with mud and silt filling every room; some were wiped off their foundations and disappeared into the rushing waters. A few of the businesses in Rapid City even saw rescue missions, as people would use the roofs of businesses to get away from the rising water. This image was taken soon after the flood, but the damage that occurred is visible. (Courtesy of the Rapid City Public Library.)

Rapid Chevrolet Co., yet another Rapid City business that was affected by the 1972 Black Hills flood, is pictured with still water in front of the building. This image was taken within a few days, if not hours, after the flooding waters went back down. (Courtesy of the Rapid City Public Library.)

Glass walls, as can be seen here on the Brekhaus Buick car dealership in Rapid City, are no match for rushing floodwaters. The water was moving so quickly that it bent the metal and shattered the glass, leaving behind a dangerous chaos. (Courtesy of the Rapid City Public Library.)

Even before the flood, Rapid City's housing commission and Pennington County recognized the need for around 300 low-cost rental units. Housing in Rapid City was limited, and the flooding made housing even more needed. It was also not the best housing—many people lived in trailers along Rapid Creek in neighborhoods sometimes referred to as "camps." (Both, courtesy of the Rapid City Public Library.)

Most homes along Rapid Creek were destroyed in the 1972 Black Hills flood. Some of them—about 200 homes—only received slight water damage due to being on the outer edges of the floodplain. These homes were not gotten rid of; instead, they were rehabilitated off the floodplain and turned into public housing for those who had been displaced by the flood. This took time; for the first year or so after the flood, many people lived in temporary housing that was available through federal means. Hotels and motels were also utilized; as mentioned earlier, people temporarily stayed at the military bases as well for a short time. Often, when houses were destroyed, people tried to get back into them and save what they could of their possessions; in cases like this, though, it would have been difficult. (Courtesy of the Rapid City Public Library.)

Homes in Rapid City faced all sorts of damage. Some received nothing more than flooded basements. Some were completely wiped off their foundations; some had so much mud and debris left inside when the floodwaters receded that the homes were declared damaged beyond repair. There were homes that were moved farther away from the floodplain and refurbished. Many families were displaced—sadly, not all who had been displaced by the floodwaters returned to, or stayed in, Rapid City. Many citizens of Rapid City left the area due to grief and loss, fear, and lack of faith in the city government. (Both, courtesy of the Rapid City Public Library.)

These homes, among many others, were taken off their foundation and moved with the floodwaters. The water moved quite quickly as well; the houses moved without warning and did not always move in one piece. When the waters receded, the homes were randomly situated. Sadly, even if the homes were intact on the outside, there was a chance the home would be demolished on the inside; the silt and mud that came with the floodwaters stuck to and destroyed everything. It was always hoped that the residents of the home would make it out before the waters swept the homes off their foundations, but that was not always the case. (Both, courtesy of the Rapid City Public Library.)

In Rapid City, the Department of Housing and Urban Development helped to fund the cost of the land needed for homes that had suffered only slight water damage but needed to be moved off the floodplain. Essentially, the homes that fit this category were able to be rehabilitated and used as housing in the future away from the floodplain. This rehabilitation of homes saved money and allowed people to potentially keep their homes. Some of the moved homes are still standing to this day. (Both, courtesy of the Rapid City Public Library.)

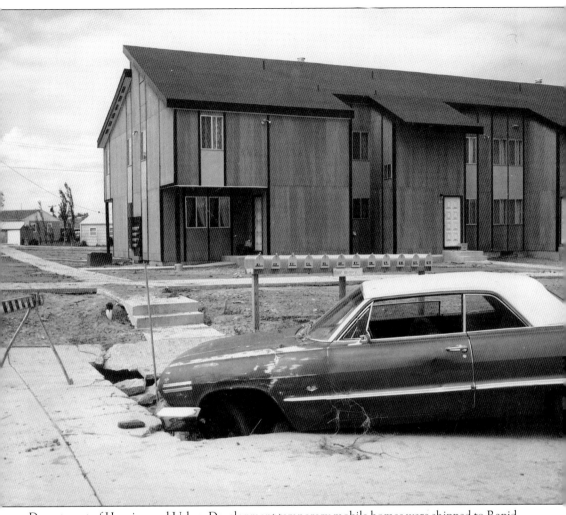

Department of Housing and Urban Development temporary mobile homes were shipped to Rapid City from other areas of South Dakota, New Mexico, Arkansas, Indiana, Wisconsin, and Kansas. As soon as the flood occurred, the governor, Richard Kneip, reached out to all the other states for aid. Some states sent funds, material goods, and volunteers; other states sent mobile homes. By August, there were 1,019 mobile homes scattered in 15 temporary trailer parks throughout the city. They provided shelter away from Rapid Creek for families that had been displaced due to the floodwaters. After the mobile homes, more permanent housing was created, as can be seen here. These more permanent houses were placed outside of the floodplain and were lower in price; some of them still exist in Rapid City today, especially in the northern area of the city. (Courtesy of the Rapid City Public Library.)

Many people who survived the flood lost everything. Their home locations, along what now is considered a floodplain, were wiped away by water and debris. If they were not wiped away, the homes would be filled with mud and water, encasing everything that people owned in thick sludge. (Courtesy of the Rapid City Public Library.)

South Dakotans were worried about the recovery of the Black Hills after the flooding because of the tourism income that came out of western South Dakota. Governor Kneip, in the early days after the flooding, issued a statement that explained the Black Hills were still open to the public, with different treks to take to get to the monuments. (Courtesy of the Rapid City Public Library.)

As mentioned before, cars ended up in unique positions when pushed around by floodwaters. Somehow, in the image to the right, this car ended up pushed up close to a concrete barrier, with the back end elevated. In this image, the car is being inspected to see if there is anyone, or anything, inside. In the below image, cars are piled on top of each other with water still surrounding them—that water stuck around for a while in the aftermath of the flooding. Heavy machinery was necessary to clean up the debris, especially if it was demolished cars. (Both, courtesy of the South Dakota National Guard.)

The citizens of Rapid City faced a major recovery process, but it did not kill their spirit. In fact, the citizens of Rapid City banded together and volunteered to help others, even if they themselves lost everything. In the secondary flood incident that occurred a week after the June 9 disaster, volunteers were out trying to help others and ended up losing their lives in the process. A group of Mennonites, who requested no recognition, spent months helping the clean-up processes in the Black Hills because they felt it was the right thing to do. Men and women gave their lives for one another in the hopes of saving a single life. The heroism and volunteerism that came out of this disaster cannot be understated; there is a reason the recovery process seemed to go quickly. This image highlights the toughness of the citizens. (Courtesy of the South Dakota National Guard.)

Many images of the night of the flood and the aftermath are passed over because they seem to be uninteresting or prove to have very little stories. This image could be considered one of those, but it depicts the hard efforts that came with the recovery process. The legs pictured here are the legs of men who responded to a specific building in the aftermath of the Black Hills flood. The building they were working in, Bennett-Clarkson Hospital, was completely damaged because of the flood, having been located right on the edge of Rapid Creek in the heart of Rapid City. This image of the mud-covered legs of responders to Bennett-Clarkson in the days after the flooding shows the efforts that the recovery personnel made to get the hospital up and running again. (Courtesy of the South Dakota National Guard.)

After the evacuation of patients and the closing of the lower floors of the hospital, all that remained at the hospital was silt, water, and debris. Many of the patients at the hospital were moved to other hospitals for care; the nurses and doctors ended up evacuating the patients in the dark of the night on June 9, 1972. This took doctors, nurses, and military and first responder personnel to do safely and quickly while keeping the patients comfortable. They were doing this while the water was still moving through the area. These actions, while they were important and saved people's lives, proved to have extra danger involved due to the floodwaters. Luckily, Rapid City had other hospitals away from Rapid Creek that could receive patients. (Courtesy of the Black Hills National Forest Historical Collection, Leland D. Case Library for Western Historical Studies, Black Hills State University.)

Three

RECOVERY IN
THE BLACK HILLS

The power of the water that came through the Black Hills cannot be understated. It had the ability to warp cars, break homes, and damage concrete. By the time the water hit Rapid City, it was moving at 50,000 cubic feet per second. (Courtesy of the Keystone Area Historical Society.)

Rapid City was not the only community affected by the 1972 Black Hills flood. Keystone, Box Elder, Nemo, and more communities in the northern Black Hills of South Dakota were affected by the flooding; their creeks flooded, their dams failed, and the roads and towns were washed out. The creeks bore the brunt of the disaster, as they were unable to handle the amount of water that came through the area on the night of June 9. The flooding started early in the evening in the northern Black Hills. (Both, courtesy of the Rapid City Public Library.)

Heavy equipment proved to be essential in the recovery processes all over the Black Hills, let alone in Rapid City. Getting the heavy equipment from area to area of the Black Hills—Rapid City to Keystone, for example—proved to be more difficult. The roads in the Black Hills were affected by the flooding as much as the creeks in that they were damaged and covered in debris, if not completely washed out. The movement of heavy vehicles depended on the accessibility of the roads, so it took longer to get the heavy vehicles around the Black Hills. This image also gives a great visual scale for the debris that was piled up; the individual on the right-hand side of the photograph is standing on top of debris that looks to be as large as he is tall. (Courtesy of the US Air Force.)

Pedestrian and vehicular bridges make up much of the Black Hills due to all the creeks that web the area. While the bridges are usually high above the creeks most of the time, these bridges were washed away during the flooding from both the floodwater itself and the debris. Luckily, as the flooding happened in the evening and late into the night, it was less likely that people would be on the bridges as they failed. The bridges in these images had less damage than the ones in Rapid City and the southern Black Hills, as there was less debris built up, but the damage was still there. (Both, courtesy of the Rapid City Public Library.)

As seen in this image, the roads of the Black Hills that were used to transport visitors and locals alike were changed after the 1972 Black Hills flood. The dirt that was washed out from under the roads made them unstable, resulting in the need to repave the roads in the hills to have the accessibility the tourists and locals had before the disaster. The roads also needed to be shaped around the creek differently in the hopes that they would be less affected by flooding the next time a disaster like this occurred. (Both, courtesy of the Rapid City Public Library.)

This is an image of what the landscape above Grizzly Bear Campground looked like after the flooding. Located near Mount Rushmore and Keystone, right along Iron Mountain Road, the campground was flooded as it was situated along Grizzly Bear Creek. The image shows how much the creek was washed out, with rocks and debris piled up unnaturally. Today, Grizzly Bear Campground still exists in the same place. The pavilion, which was built by the Civilian Conservation Corps and was flooded as well, survived the flood and can still be used. No fatalities occurred at this campground—luckily all the campers who were there got away from the rising waters in time. This, and many other aerial photographs, were taken right after the flooding occurred to see the breadth of the damage. (Courtesy of the Black Hills National Forest Historical Collection, Leland D. Case Library for Western Historical Studies, Black Hills State University.)

There were, and still are, many dams in the Black Hills. This image shows the area above Victoria Dam, which was damaged the night of the flood. Victoria Dam was a concrete dam that was utilized with Victoria Lake, which was between Hisega to the north and Rockerville to the south. Victoria Dam needed to be repaired a couple of times after the flooding occurred, but eventually, Victoria Lake was drained and never refilled. When this happened, the dam was ultimately removed. This image shows Victoria Creek, which was blown out from the floodwaters. The banks and trees seen in the image are much more beat up because of the water than they would have been prior to the flood. (Courtesy of the Black Hills National Forest Historical Collection, Leland D. Case Library for Western Historical Studies, Black Hills State University.)

This is an image after the flood of the Alkali Creek area, which is located near Sturgis, South Dakota. The information from the Black Hills National Forest Historical Collection states that located in this image are the weirs and gauging stations, both of which were damaged during the flooding. Alkali Creek is a popular place, as it has trailheads that are part of the Centennial Trail and multiple picnic areas, as well as options for camping and an RV park, all of which were affected by the flooding in 1972. In this image, one can see the damage the water has done to the creek; the blown-out creek bed looks very different in this image than the ones taken prior to the flooding. (Courtesy of the Black Hills National Forest Historical Collection, Leland D. Case Library for Western Historical Studies, Black Hills State University.)

Bitter Creek Campground, seen in this image, was wiped away after the flood. This image highlights the damage, with the open ground that was an occupied campground. A lone building can be seen still standing, though it is unclear from this image what kind of damage was done to that building. The creek banks were blown out from the overwhelming amount of water that rushed through the area; this is visible in the photograph. Located between Rapid City and Mount Rushmore, Bitter Creek branches off from Spring Creek; both creeks were affected by the flooding. It was named after the bitter taste the water in the creek carries. The creek still exists in the Black Hills. (Courtesy of the Black Hills National Forest Historical Collection, Leland D. Case Library for Western Historical Studies, Black Hills State University.)

This image of the damage that was done to the Battle Creek Picnic Ground after the flooding highlights the movement of the recovery process. The image shows vehicle marks where heavy machinery moved around to clean up the area. (Courtesy of the Black Hills National Forest Historical Collection, Leland D. Case Library for Western Historical Studies, Black Hills State University.)

The signage in this image is pointing visitors toward the Battle Creek Campground, which was completely wiped out during the flood. Located near Hermosa, South Dakota, this was a popular campground for visitors to the Black Hills. The foreground of the image gives an idea of what kind of damage was done at the campground. (Courtesy of the Keystone Area Historical Society.)

Boxelder Forks Campground, located about a mile and a half from Nemo, South Dakota, was also affected by the flooding. Located in the northern Black Hills, this campground was an area that was flooded early on the night of June 9, 1972, when Boxelder Creek flooded with rainwater. Boxelder Creek runs past the campground, and the proximity to the creek, as well as the remote area the campground is in, is still promoted as an attraction for people to use this campground over other campgrounds in the Black Hills. In this image, the tracks in the mud that are visible are from the heavy machinery used for clean-up in the aftermath. The area looked much different before the flooding. (Courtesy of the Black Hills National Forest Historical Collection, Leland D. Case Library for Western Historical Studies, Black Hills State University.)

This image, taken after the flooding occurred, shows the second and third Sturgis reservoirs, with the second at the top of the image and the third one below; a bridge has been knocked out between the two. The lack of a bridge means that the waters took it out when they overstretched the banks of the reservoir. It also shows the blown-out area of the third reservoir. The white area in the image did not exist there to that extent before the flood; the water that rushed through the reservoir caused that area. The reservoirs, and their corresponding dams, were greatly affected by the 1972 Black Hills flood. Today, they are accessible for hiking and fishing. (Courtesy of the Black Hills National Forest Historical Collection, Leland D. Case Library for Western Historical Studies, Black Hills State University.)

Dalton Dam, while still standing after the flood, was very damaged due to the waters. As seen in this image, the dam was surrounded by debris and had a lot of erosion around it from the waters. Started in 1934 and finished in 1937, this dam is still standing today. The need for a lot of repairs to the face of the dam in the days and months after the flooding was high. Little Elk Creek, which feeds the lake that the dam sits on, experienced damage from the flooding on the night of June 9. Dalton Dam, and Dalton Lake, are located near Nemo, South Dakota. (Courtesy of the Black Hills National Forest Historical Collection, Leland D. Case Library for Western Historical Studies, Black Hills State University.)

The dam at Deer Creek Campground faced a lot of damage after the flooding. This image clearly shows the damage to the dam itself as well as where the water rushed through with the bank erosion below the dam. It looks as though when this image was taken after the flood, water was still running through the damaged dam; this would have been a regulated action before the flooding occurred. It is unclear how badly the campground was affected by the flooding from this image, but it can be inferred that the campground suffered water damage if it was like the other campgrounds affected by the flooding in the Black Hills. Deer Creek Campground is far into the Black Hills, 15 miles away from Rapid City, and is a part of the Centennial Trail. The campground was located right along Deer Creek. (Courtesy of the Black Hills National Forest Historical Collection, Leland D. Case Library for Western Historical Studies, Black Hills State University.)

Debris build-up was a threat to stream-gaging stations as well as bridges, roads, and dams. This image was likely taken after the flooding on June 9, 1972, near Nemo, South Dakota. There were many of these systems set up in the Black Hills before the flooding occurred, and they did gather a lot of information about the floodwaters before they were damaged or destroyed by overwhelming water. These had to be inspected thoroughly in the days and weeks after the flooding occurred to see whether they could be reused in the future or would need to be replaced. Today, there are still stream gauges with alarm systems in the Black Hills creeks to help mitigate threats like what happened in 1972. (Courtesy of the Black Hills National Forest Historical Collection, Leland D. Case Library for Western Historical Studies, Black Hills State University.)

This view of an overflow of water emphasizes how much water came through. This creek was overfilled to the point where water was coming up and surrounding the plants and trees on the banks. (Courtesy of the Black Hills National Forest Historical Collection, Leland D. Case Library for Western Historical Studies, Black Hills State University.)

Horsethief Dam, and the lake behind the dam, were created in the 1930s by the Civilian Conservation Corps. Located quite close to Mount Rushmore, the dam was damaged during the flooding—this image shows some of the damage. (Courtesy of the Black Hills National Forest Historical Collection, Leland D. Case Library for Western Historical Studies, Black Hills State University.)

Erosion of creek banks was a major issue in the aftermath of the flood and needed to be quickly mitigated—so much so that organizations would measure the erosion pedestals. The above image is a close-up view of erosion that had occurred; the image below shows one of the markers that measures where the top of the bank was versus where it eroded. These markers ended up littering the creeks in the Black Hills because of the extensive erosion damage. (Both, courtesy of the Black Hills National Forest Historical Collection, Leland D. Case Library for Western Historical Studies, Black Hills State University.)

Both of these images highlight the damage done to the Homestake Dam group after the flooding was completed on June 9, 1972. With the debris that came through the dams, it is amazing that they were not damaged more; the building-up debris, including trees, can be seen in both images. Both dams were used originally to help power parts of the Homestake Mine in Lead. They needed to be mended almost immediately to not slow down the mining production of the area. (Both, courtesy of the Black Hills National Forest Historical Collection, Leland D. Case Library for Western Historical Studies, Black Hills State University.)

A popular place to visit today, Lakota Dam and Lakota Lake, located southeast of Keystone, South Dakota, were damaged by floodwaters and debris as well. This image shows the aftermath of the water running through the area and knocking trees over. It is likely that many of the trees surrounding the dam and the lake made it down to Rapid City, where a lot of the damage from the flooding occurred. The dam was not able to hold back the rushing water that came through the area. Many of these dams are in remote areas, where accessing them was easier through aerial means rather than wheeled means, especially after a disaster that took out many bridges and blew out creek beds. (Courtesy of the Black Hills National Forest Historical Collection, Leland D. Case Library for Western Historical Studies, Black Hills State University.)

Fort Meade Dam, pictured here, faced a lot of damage on the night of June 9, 1972. The erosion and damage that the floodwaters caused are quite visible in this image. After the flood, according to a report by the US Army Corps of Engineers, one of the segments of the dam had to be purposely exploded to stop the possibility of the dam's collapse if there was another flooding event. There was a very real worry that if the dam collapsed, an estimated seven million gallons of water would make its way to Sturgis and do extensive damage to the town. The damage caused the Community Hospital to be evacuated until it could be inspected. Today, the dam holds back Fort Meade Reservoir, a small lake located near Sturgis, South Dakota. (Courtesy of the Black Hills National Forest Historical Collection, Leland D. Case Library for Western Historical Studies, Black Hills State University.)

This is Sheridan Lake Dam post-flood. All the areas of the Black Hills that were affected by the flooding were either rebuilt stronger and better or were later completely taken apart. Sheridan Lake still exists, as does the dam, but the same cannot be said for all the dams that failed because of the flooding. (Courtesy of the Black Hills National Forest Historical Collection, Leland D. Case Library for Western Historical Studies, Black Hills State University.)

Sheridan Lake, a popular fishing spot, is located about 15 miles west of Rapid City, deeper in the Black Hills. This image shows the north cove of Sheridan Lake and how it was completely washed out after the flooding occurred. (Courtesy of the Black Hills National Forest Historical Collection, Leland D. Case Library for Western Historical Studies, Black Hills State University.)

This image shows the aftermath of the flood at the Pactola Work Center. Once a ranger station in the Black Hills, this image highlights the desolation of the water rushing through the area. (Courtesy of the Black Hills National Forest Historical Collection, Leland D. Case Library for Western Historical Studies, Black Hills State University.)

The Boxelder Civilian Conservation Center, located near Nemo, South Dakota, was only slightly affected by the flooding—some debris made its way toward the center. However, the flood gave the corpsmen an opportunity to help the surrounding areas and move the Black Hills toward recovery. (Courtesy of the Black Hills National Forest Historical Collection, Leland D. Case Library for Western Historical Studies, Black Hills State University.)

This image highlights the efforts that were put forth to protect civilians from the damages of the flood in the aftermath. In the background of the image, roadblocks are up in the hopes of stopping travelers on the road, as the culvert that was left there had not been moved yet. (Courtesy of the Black Hills National Forest Historical Collection, Leland D. Case Library for Western Historical Studies, Black Hills State University.)

Other times, humans will do something dangerous with very little prompting. This gully, formed by the floodwaters and most likely a deep and dangerous area, needed to be explored for debris and depth. (Courtesy of the Black Hills National Forest Historical Collection, Leland D. Case Library for Western Historical Studies, Black Hills State University.)

Here is another example of a bridge being damaged and needing repairs due to debris in the floodwaters after the 1972 Black Hills flood. This is Davenport's Bridge in the Black Hills. (Courtesy of the Black Hills National Forest Historical Collection, Leland D. Case Library for Western Historical Studies, Black Hills State University.)

This stone structure is believed to be an abutment to a bridge that was demolished by the 1972 Black Hills flood. The location is guessed to be near Gingrass Draw. (Courtesy of the Black Hills National Forest Historical Collection, Leland D. Case Library for Western Historical Studies, Black Hills State University.)

This ranch, located on Estes Creek, saw the aftermath of the flooding with the debris and piles of rocks that came through the property. On the left side of this image is standing water from the flooding. It is not clear from this image whether the floodwaters reached the ranch house itself and what damage, if any, was done to the home; however, the space near the ranch house suggests that floodwaters did make it up close to the home, if not inside. That open space seems to be washed-out dirt instead of a purposeful space for driving or other movements. Estes Creek, and this ranch, are located right outside of Nemo, South Dakota. Much of the flooding in this area happened earlier in the night than when it occurred in Rapid City, South Dakota. (Courtesy of the Black Hills National Forest Historical Collection, Leland D. Case Library for Western Historical Studies, Black Hills State University.)

Spring Creek Campground was washed out due to the flooding in the Black Hills. In this photograph, the damage to the bridge across Spring Creek is very clear; by the time this image had been taken, the bridge had not even been approached for being repaired yet. The upper part of the image also shows damage to the banks of Spring Creek; the water overflow ate away at the dirt and plants, causing this area to now look barren in comparison to the surrounding Black Hills land. The road in this picture was also most likely washed out from the flooding, though it does not show too much damage in this image. This area, again a secluded campground, is about eight miles southwest of Rapid City. (Courtesy of the Black Hills National Forest Historical Collection, Leland D. Case Library for Western Historical Studies, Black Hills State University.)

The recovery process in Keystone was very similar to the recovery process in other parts of the Black Hills. The dump trucks in the foreground of this image are lined up in preparation for removing debris from this area of Keystone. Being a tourist town, these signs show the businesses that were directly affected by the flooding. (Courtesy of the Keystone Area Historical Society.)

This pile of debris was in Keystone, across from the Bullion. The signage behind the debris is a poignant reminder of what was lost during the 1972 Black Hills flood and what survived. The Black Hills continued to be beautiful, just changed because of the disaster. (Courtesy of the Keystone Area Historical Society.)

This debris was once a bridge near First and Madill Streets in Keystone, South Dakota. The bridge was wiped out by the floodwaters rushing through Keystone, and the car in the background was set there by the water. (Courtesy of the Keystone Area Historical Society.)

This image looks east down what was Swanzey Street in Keystone, South Dakota. The railroad used to follow along Swanzey Street, but the floodwaters did irreparable damage to the railroad tracks that these individuals are walking along. It is not quite clear what they are looking for here—it could be anything from fatalities to specific types of debris to what kind of work would be needed to fix the track. (Courtesy of the Keystone Area Historical Society.)

The Keystone Fire Department was directly affected by the flood since it was on Reed Street when the flooding occurred. The mud from the flooding got into the garage, making it difficult to get the vehicles out, as well as the water that may have done damage to them. Today, what was the Keystone Fire Department is now the Battle Creek Lodge. It is still along the creek, where all the flooding occurred in 1972. (Both, courtesy of the Keystone Area Historical Society.)

The summer of 1972 was one full of tourists camping in the Black Hills. This image highlights exactly what people were doing: traveling to Keystone until they were stopped by the debris of the flood. There is a similar sign in Keystone today pointing tourists and visitors to all of the highlights that the area has to offer. (Courtesy of the Keystone Area Historical Society.)

The South Dakota Highway Patrol has multiple stories from the flooding in 1972 that highlight the efforts it undertook to keep people safe—sometimes to its own failure. In this case, the story is told that this trooper was attempting to warn Keystone residents of the rising water and got stuck; his lights were flashing throughout the night of June 9, 1972. (Courtesy of the Keystone Area Historical Society.)

This image shows what was left between Swanzey and Reed Streets after the flooding occurred in Keystone. The far background shows cars that are balancing on top of debris, having been placed there by the waters. No one really realized what water could do to vehicles until the floodwaters came through. The far background also shows a few buildings that were affected by the floodwaters—mostly the silt and mud that they transported as they moved through Keystone. The foreground shows standing water, much of which was in the same place for a few days, if not a full week, after the flood. After that, the mud that was caused by the standing water proved to be more of an issue, as it would cake on everything. (Courtesy of the Keystone Area Historical Society.)

These images highlight how much damage was done on Reed Street in Keystone, South Dakota. Taken looking toward the east on Reed Street, these images not only show the mud that was left behind from the water but also the water itself. The water caused issues in the form of hiding debris and could potentially have caused health issues had there not been an active push for recovery directly after the flood. The standing water also attracted insect swarms, which, in the height of summer, could prove to be more dangerous than many other threats in the Black Hills. (Both, courtesy of the Keystone Area Historical Society.)

This is the bend at Reed and First Streets in Keystone. This image was taken soon after the floodwaters receded, as there was still standing water at the time this image was taken. These individuals were walking along the road, looking at the damage and searching for debris, bodies, and more. The standing water was not entered unless the search party was dressed safely and it was necessary to enter the water; otherwise, search parties would use other means of looking and exploring the areas where visibility was cut down. This image also shows erosion in the road, which was fixed before the road was reopened for the tourists in the Black Hills. The floodwaters ate away the soil under the pavement, causing the pavement to crumble and fall away from the road. (Courtesy of the Keystone Area Historical Society.)

This image is looking south on Winter Street in Keystone, South Dakota. The depth of the damage can be seen here. The layers of debris, the washed-out roads and creek beds, and the damaged buildings are all extremely obvious. In fact, quite visible is the erosion of the roads, as well as the cracking of the pavement in some areas. It also reiterates the strength that the survivors had in the face of disaster; these individuals are most likely saddened by what happened but are also figuring out how to move forward with resiliency. (Courtesy of the Keystone Area Historical Society.)

The entrance to Rushmore Mine was damaged in the flood. Keystone was, and still is, a major tourist attraction because of its proximity to Mount Rushmore. The damage that the flood caused made it difficult for tourists to access the town for days after the flood. (Courtesy of Keystone Area Historical Society.)

The South Dakota National Guard did not only respond to Rapid City. As soon as it could get to the town of Keystone, it brought equipment to start cleaning up the debris that littered the community. The dump truck pictured here, among many other vehicles and tools, proved to be invaluable. (Courtesy of the Rapid City Public Library.)

These two images are of the same pile of debris from different angles. The pile of debris was located near the Borglum Story in Keystone, South Dakota, placed there after the floodwaters receded. Not only does it show the ability of water to move vehicles, it also shows the ability of the water to damage, dent, and bend metal. The plant debris was wedged between the metal by the waters rushing through. Interestingly, it was not realized that these images were of the same pile of debris until a closer look was taken—the Volkswagen bus gave it away. (Both, courtesy of Keystone Area Historical Society.)

The Ruby House Restaurant, a staple in Keystone, faced some major damage after the floodwaters receded. Mud and silt, pushed along by the water, were in layers along the floor. The silt and other debris left behind from the flooding can also be seen in front of the restaurant. It took months to clean out the restaurant. (Courtesy of the Keystone Area Historical Society.)

Some of the buildings in Keystone did not survive the flooding. The ones that were close to the creek were most susceptible to receiving damage that completely obliterated them, moving them off their foundations and downstream. (Courtesy of the Black Hills National Forest Historical Collection, Leland D. Case Library for Western Historical Studies, Black Hills State University.)

The damage seen here was found on Swanzey Street after floodwaters receded. Multiple citizens of Keystone ended up helping with the recovery efforts of Keystone, including inspecting the railroad tracks, as that was a main mode of transportation of goods through the Black Hills. Losing a set of railroad tracks damaged by floodwaters caused issues for the railroad and prompted the rebuilding of the railroad and the town of Keystone. Sadly, eight lives were lost in and around Keystone; this number is included in the over 200 listed on memorials around the Black Hills. (Both, courtesy of the Keystone Area Historical Society.)

Accessing towns in the Black Hills proved to be more difficult than originally imagined. When bridges, like the one pictured here, are blown out beyond temporary repair, more creative avenues of movement were taken, including sending men over on foot to climb the debris and get to the other side. (Courtesy of the Rapid City Public Library.)

Luckily, the heavy machinery that the South Dakota National Guard and other organizations had allowed for the rebuilding of bridges and other damaged areas easily. Here, the National Guard is towing debris to clear the way for the movement of personnel and, as seen in the image, the pumping of standing water. (Courtesy of the South Dakota National Guard.)

The image above is of a debris disposal site, an area out of the way that would not become filled quickly. Here, one can see heavy machinery, including dump trucks, pushing the debris around to utilize all the space in the disposal area. The land that was cleaned needed to be coaxed into regrowth—including the plant life that was killed in the flood, as seen below. (Both, courtesy of the Rapid City Public Library.)

Driving around the Black Hills is a wonderful pastime, even without visiting the monuments and going for hikes. If, however, access to the Black Hills was prevented—as seen in this image—then there would have to be other routes to take. This overpass was damaged from the flooding and closed to vehicles. Driving over this overpass could prove to be dangerous without it being inspected, as seen in this image. The water damage done below the overpass, where the dark areas are in the picture, could indicate upturned soil and weakness in the columns. Although not a total loss, it is important to remember that even the bridges that looked fine after the flood could have minute cracking and issues that would need to be repaired; otherwise, the cracks could grow bigger and become more dangerous with time. (Courtesy of the Rapid City Public Library.)

This damage was caused by the flooding, though the location is not quite clear. The desolation of the image is striking; the empty, rock-ridden foreground and the pile of debris in the background highlight the sadness of the disaster. It also needs to be noted that these images, while helpful in describing the magnitude of the disaster, do not give a lot of other information. The scale in this image is not helpful, as the trees in the background are not fully in the image; there is no indication of what is on the ground; and the debris itself is so mangled that without getting up close to it, there is no real ability to tell what it is. This is a building, but not every image is as easy to tell. (Courtesy of the Rapid City Public Library.)

Four

THE PEOPLE OF THE FLOOD

The disaster of the 1972 Black Hills flood brought people together. Due to the damages done to homes and businesses, the citizens of the Black Hills faced homelessness, a lack of basic needs, and an overall sense of tragedy. The survivors of the disaster banded together to make the recovery occur. (Courtesy of the Rapid City Public Library.)

Citizens of the Black Hills stepped up in the recovery process as soon as the sun dawned on June 10. Pictured is a man walking the debris left behind from damaged concrete—it could be from a failed dam, or the foundation of a building—and many individuals did a similar action over the following months. It is unclear what he is searching for; he could be checking for failure points in the concrete, debris, fatalities, or many other things. These inspections allowed the governments—local, federal, and state—to decide what kind of response was needed to the disaster as well as the monetary funds that were needed for said response. In this case, an immediate and all-encompassing response was necessary. (Courtesy of the Black Hills National Forest Historical Collection, Leland D. Case Library for Western Historical Studies, Black Hills State University.)

This image shows men inspecting what looks to be a bridge for damage from floodwaters, and the debris to the left side of the image was probably shocking to the inspectors. No one expected the disaster to be what it was. What is lucky for the Black Hills is that the South Dakota National Guard was in training during the week prior to the flooding. Usually, the soldiers of the South Dakota National Guard are spread across the state; only once a year, at the time of the flooding, were they all in one place for training. They ended up being a huge boon to the Black Hills, through performing inspections, helping the clean-up processes, search and rescue, fatality recovery, and more. (Courtesy of the Black Hills National Forest Historical Collection, Leland D. Case Library for Western Historical Studies, Black Hills State University.)

The man staring at the camera in this image is Edwald Hayes, a well-known individual in Keystone who survived the flooding. It is not clear if he was posing for the camera or if the camera person caught him at the right moment, but this is one of the clearest images of someone from Keystone that exists in relation to the 1972 Black Hills flood. The background of the image is looking up Highway 16A, which took tourists to Rapid City as well as Mount Rushmore. The cars built up are both tourists and locals who were trying to make it into or through Keystone. It can be assumed that some of the individuals in those cars were coming into Keystone to make sure that the people of Keystone were okay. Today, this road looks much the same and is traveled quite often by individuals trying to get to Mount Rushmore. (Courtesy of the Keystone Area Historical Society.)

While dangerous, walking through standing water after the flood was a necessary action. These actions were done to search for fatalities from the flood as well as to clear debris to rebuild the area. In the background of the top image, damaged cars and heavy equipment can be seen, a dichotomy that really indicates what the recovery of the flood was like. The men in the image below prepare to clean the bridge of debris but are also inspecting the area below the bridge for other debris or, sadly, fatalities from the flooding. (Above, courtesy of the Rapid City Public Library; below, courtesy of the South Dakota National Guard.)

Fatality recovery was difficult. At some point after the 1972 Black Hills flood, the efforts of search and rescue turned into recovery. It was also necessary to do fatality recovery to help with the clean-up of the area, as the decomposition of bodies can affect water quality, cause animal problems, and impact the mental health of the community. With over 200 people dying in a tragedy, the mental health of a community took precedence over many other worries; while only a fraction of the population of the Black Hills, the fatality list seems to hold some of the most well-known individuals of the area. (Above, courtesy of the Rapid City Public Library; below, courtesy of the South Dakota National Guard.)

The 1972 Black Hills flood caused worry across the nation. Sen. George McGovern, who is pictured here in the suit and tie, immediately responded to the Black Hills, coming out to visit and meet with the local community leaders. He was in the middle of a presidential race, which he would end up losing to Pres. Richard M. Nixon. McGovern went on to push for bills to pass in Congress that created flood-related laws to prevent disasters of this magnitude from occurring again, especially in the Black Hills. Nixon and McGovern ended up disagreeing about many policies, including the flood response in South Dakota. In this image, Col. J.B. Reed of Ellsworth Air Force Base is showing Senator McGovern the recovery process and what Ellsworth Air Force Base was doing to help the recovery process. (Courtesy of the US Air Force.)

Col. J.B. Reed was not aware of what the night of June 9 would bring for him and the base that he oversaw. As wing commander of Ellsworth Air Force Base, he was more worried about the missile silos that Ellsworth oversaw, the bombers that the base housed, and the men he oversaw every single day. He went on to allow Ellsworth Air Force Base to open the gates to individuals in need in the aftermath of the flood, oversee the recovery and searching processes that his men would be a part of, and be the one to honor his men who died during the flood while trying to save others from the floodwaters. The flooding that occurred proved to be another test that he faced in his time at Ellsworth Air Force Base. (Courtesy of the US Air Force.)

One of the most incredible takeaways from the 1972 Black Hills flood was the cooperation that state, local, and federal entities had during and after the disaster. FEMA was not created at the time of the 1972 Black Hills flood, and so the creation of an emergency management team that included Ellsworth Air Force Base, the South Dakota National Guard, and local first responders was ahead of its time. The Emergency Operations Center, or EOC as it was known, also made sure to communicate with the mayor of Rapid City, Don Barnett, to keep him posted on what areas of Rapid City were having more flooding than others. (Above, courtesy of the US Air Force; below, courtesy of the South Dakota National Guard.)

The men who manned the emergency management task force worked long days before they could get a break. Many of them had families directly affected by the flooding, and yet they made sure they were doing their jobs too. Without the organization in all the chaos, many more lives would have been lost. Their efforts were not completely done when the flood itself was over; with thousands of volunteers flocking into the Black Hills, the organization of people was needed and extremely important. All these men were able to organize and utilize the volunteers in the best possible way. (Both, courtesy of the South Dakota National Guard.)

Ellsworth Air Force Base personnel escort Sen. George McGovern and other dignitaries to a helicopter, from which they were able to see the damage that the 1972 Black Hills flood had done to the area surrounding the base. They flew over the Black Hills and the creeks therein, making sure to find where all the damage was done and what was needed. Other dignitaries that came to the Black Hills in the aftermath of the flood included Gov. Richard Kneip, Vice Pres. Spiro T. Agnew, and First Lady Pat Nixon. While all came out here with different plans and ideas in mind—Vice President Agnew came out with news of funding for the Black Hills, for example—they were all impressed with the efforts that occurred and how well people banded together in the aftermath of the disaster. (Courtesy of the US Air Force.)

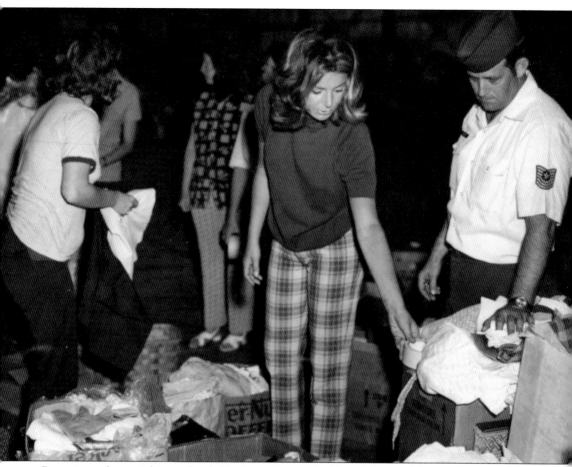

Donations of material items flooded in from all over the United States of America and needed to be sorted. Personnel from Ellsworth Air Force Base, along with volunteers, helped sort the items, which included clothing, medicine, water, food, and more necessities that Rapid City and the surrounding Black Hills citizens needed. (Courtesy of the US Air Force.)

In Rapid City, grocery stores that were not damaged by the flood ended up opening their doors and giving food to the hospital, which was still actively working. The American Red Cross was available, as was the Salvation Army. These two organizations, and others, were essential in the recovery of the Black Hills. (Courtesy of the US Air Force.)

These men, wearing hard hats and work overalls, prepare to clean up the debris that was left behind from the 1972 Black Hills flood. Armed with what look to be power washers, the men ended up spending a lot of time clearing silt and debris from the communities in the Black Hills. They could also be preparing to spray pesticides along the standing water that was left in the towns and along the roads in the Black Hills. These men ended up working nonstop side by side with first responders, military personnel, and other volunteers, as well as their fellow community members. The communities paid them back with kindness; food and water were easy to get when they were working so hard to recover the Black Hills from the disaster. (Courtesy of the South Dakota National Guard.)

This image highlights the movement of debris by humans in the aftermath of the flood. It took three men to pull this debris out of the way, indicating that it was either a large piece of house or a large piece of metal. The men are wearing hard hats and gloves so that they stay safe during debris clean-up, and it makes sense considering the threats of falling debris as well as tetanus and other potentially harmful threats that linger in the debris. In the background are several trucks that were used for debris clean-up, as well as what could be a heavy equipment vehicle in the very far background. Along the right-hand side of the image, the erosion of the road is visible. (Courtesy of the Black Hills National Forest Historical Collection, Leland D. Case Library for Western Historical Studies, Black Hills State University.)

Sometimes, people do not realize the extent of the damage to an area until they can see it for themselves. Many of the images that were taken in the aftermath of the flooding were to help understand the disaster better and to allow the after-action reports to be written with more accuracy. The other thing that occurs with major disasters such as the 1972 Black Hills flood is that the human mind cannot always comprehend what it has experienced and seen. Images like this one will help prompt the survivors of the flood to remember what they experienced for their reports and stories in the future. This image, with the person in the foreground to give perspective, highlights how much damage the flooding did in the Black Hills. The enormity of the situation was often crushing. (Courtesy of the South Dakota National Guard.)

The City of Rapid City asked the federal government for $65 million, of which it received $48 million, for longer-term housing for Rapid City citizens and the purchasing of properties that had been flooded. Vice President Agnew came to visit the area and bring the news of the money coming from the federal government, a huge boon to Rapid City. By purchasing these properties that had previously flooded, citizens were moved away from the potential future flooding of the creek. This came from a group of individuals, the council members at the time, who knew that this would not be a one-off disaster and that there would always be a chance of another flood. The property in this image was likely one of the ones that were bought and turned into greenspaces in Rapid City—either a golf course or a park for the future citizens of Rapid City. (Courtesy of the Rapid City Public Library.)

Forty-eight homes, also known as units, were approved for removal and rehabilitation on July 6, 1973, a little over a year after the flood occurred. When they were completely rehabilitated, each unit cost an average of $35,228—a very affordable rate at the time. The Department of Housing and Urban Development also worked on programs to provide subsidized housing for eligible low-income families in the aftermath of the flood. But not everyone wanted to leave their homes to move somewhere completely different and new. Even when the flooding was happening, many people did not want to evacuate their homes and get out of the flooding waters because they did not think it was going to happen as badly as it did. Human nature seems to indicate that people are stubborn about what they are supposed to do; moving out of a deadly floodplain would be smart but was not always happily done. (Courtesy of the Rapid City Public Library.)

The sadness visible on this woman's face highlights the trauma that came with the 1972 Black Hills flood. In the many reports that were submitted in the weeks and months after the flood, a few were from the Department of Social Services, churches, and mental health professionals that highlighted worries about the mental health of the community. Some individuals gave up their families and their children because they felt that they were unable to protect them since they could not protect them from the flooding. There was a worry that alcoholism and drug use would rise in the aftermath of the flooding as despair took over. And for those who lost loved ones or all their material goods, or knew someone who lost, the sadness and the grief were overwhelming. There was also hope; the federal government funding and the cooperation of everyday people were huge steps forward toward a successful recovery. (Courtesy of the South Dakota National Guard.)

The official number of deaths from the 1972 Black Hills flood is 238. This does include the 5 missing individuals whose bodies were never found. Other research indicates that there were more fatalities; the numbers depend on the definition of a "flood-related death." Either way, at least 238 people died in the 1972 Black Hills flood. By the end of June 10, almost 200 fatalities had been found. The funeral homes in Rapid City banded together and created a nonprofit organization to fund the mortuary services for all the fatalities of the flooding; pastors and priests of the local churches worked together to give multiple services a day. A large memorial service was held within the first week of the flood with some dignitaries attending the ceremony as well. This image is of soldiers retrieving a fatality of the flood, braving the standing and moving water to retrieve the body. (Courtesy of the South Dakota National Guard.)

Soldiers and airmen proved to be invaluable in the recovery of the flooding. This image shows men searching or clearing debris of what looks to be trailer homes, most likely in Rapid City. There were large amounts of trailer homes right along Rapid Creek before the flooding occurred on June 9. The helmets look to be the ones that they were issued for military service, rather than hard hats—this is likely because there were not enough hard hats to pass out to all volunteers. In fact, many of the volunteers who came to help with the recovery from the flooding most likely did not have the right gear for the actions they were carrying out. The man in the background is only wearing a baseball cap; this just highlights the different gear that the men had during the recovery process. (Courtesy of the South Dakota National Guard.)

This image shows men who are part of the 200th Engineering Company building an M4T6 bridge across Rapid Creek, most likely to move equipment, on June 12. This temporary bridge proved to be helpful as recovery processes continued, as both people and vehicles needed to get from one side of Rapid City to the other; Rapid Creek runs through the middle of the city, and when it flooded, it separated the two sides. Heavy equipment, separated families, and organizations giving recovery response to the flooding wanted to move across town. The South Dakota National Guard units were well trained in building bridges, as that was often what they ended up doing in training and when they were deployed overseas. Today, the South Dakota National Guard still hosts an annual training in the Black Hills. (Courtesy of the South Dakota National Guard.)

These men, working with the 109th Engineering Battalion and the Corps of Engineers, work on reinforcing Fort Meade Dam in the aftermath of the flooding. The Army Corps of Engineers was another one of the responding groups in the aftermath of the flooding. They proved to be invaluable with their research and data that was gathered on the dams throughout the Black Hills and what needed to be done to rebuild them safely. Walking across the top of the dam, the individuals in this image were able to see all the debris and damage that was done to both the dam and the reservoir. This image also shows the varied debris that was pushed downstream from the flooding in the northern part of the Black Hills. Tires, metal, wood, and plants were all items that were picked up and moved because of the flooding. (Courtesy of the South Dakota National Guard.)

These Boxelder Corpsmen had their picture taken on June 15, 1972. They had just been bussed in to help with the clean-up process, most likely in Keystone, South Dakota. They were later sent to Rapid City and other areas of the Black Hills as well. Dressed in hard hats, work boots, and overalls, these men were on the front lines of the clean-up processes. They worked long days, multiple days in a row, trying to help the area recover. (Both, courtesy of the Black Hills National Forest Historical Collection, Leland D. Case Library for Western Historical Studies, Black Hills State University.)

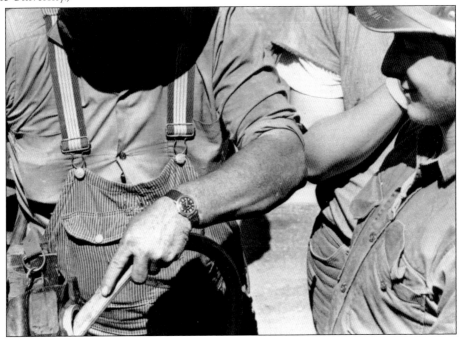

These four men are pulling up damaged flooring in a building in Keystone. While it is not clear what building they are in, the damage that the water did to the building is very visible. Had the flooring not been pulled up, there is also a high likelihood that there would be mold growing in and on the flooring at some point in the future. The thought of mold needed to be considered with every building that was affected in the Black Hills due to flooding; the mud and silt also damaged flooring until it was beyond saving as well. The child behind them, with the crutches, looks on as they work on recovery from the floodwaters that rushed through the town. Hard hats, work gloves, and coveralls are all visible in this image. (Courtesy of the Black Hills National Forest Historical Collection, Leland D. Case Library for Western Historical Studies, Black Hills State University.)

These men are surrounding a truck in Keystone that has what looks like an apparatus on it for spraying insects. With the standing water and mud in the area, the threat of insect populations, like mosquitos, increasing was very high. These men worked on decreasing the possibility of the birth of insects by spraying the area with pesticides. They also worked on slowly pumping the standing water out of the area. With the technology that was had in 1972, recovery processes were slower than the recovery processes would be today. Even getting pesticides to be sprayed was something that was waited for; there was no real way all that pesticide was available and on-hand. (Courtesy of the Black Hills National Forest Historical Collection, Leland D. Case Library for Western Historical Studies, Black Hills State University.)

This image is of a building in Keystone that was damaged by the 1972 Black Hills flood. While it is not clear what building this is, it is assumed it was one quite close to the creek because of all the debris along the floor. The men in the image are Boxelder Corpsmen who are helping with the clean-up processes. They were bussed into Keystone to help with the recovery processes a few days after the flooding had occurred. In the foreground of the image, the debris buildup is visible. Also visible are the bricks that were ripped apart either by the flooding or by humans after the flooding for ease of access. (Courtesy of the Black Hills National Forest Historical Collection, Leland D. Case Library for Western Historical Studies, Black Hills State University.)

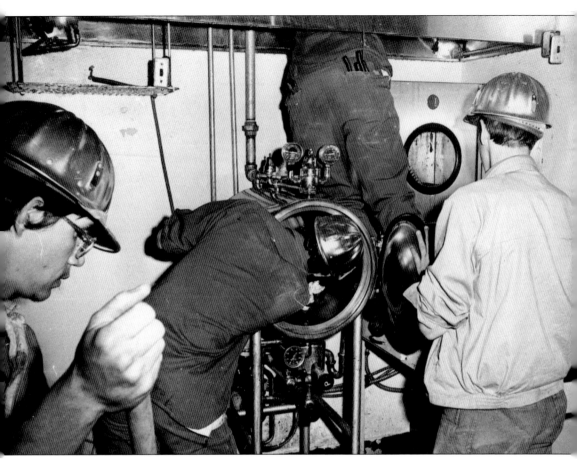

Bennett-Clarkson Hospital lost power and needed to evacuate the patients situated there during the 1972 Black Hills flood. This image shows Boxelder Corpsmen making their way to the hospital and aiding in the recovery, including doing maintenance. Maintenance at the hospital consisted of getting electricity back to the building, making sure the water was still flowing, and ensuring that the machines with lifesaving capabilities still worked. Visible in the foreground is still the reminder that the floors of the hospital were covered in mud and silt. While it is not clear whether the tool is a shovel, a broom, or a mop, the man in the foreground was doing important work and helping navigate the recovery processes. (Courtesy of the Black Hills National Forest Historical Collection, Leland D. Case Library for Western Historical Studies, Black Hills State University.)

The Boxelder Corpsmen made their way to Rapid City as well and helped in the clean-up processes there. Men in both images mop up the water and mud that was left in Bennett-Clarkson Hospital after the flooding occurred. While a seemingly menial task, anything that would help the recovery process was important. Many of the people who participated in the clean-up processes were recognized for their volunteerism. Many of the military personnel were given medals for their service or other awards. The volunteers also received the recognition that they were helpful, and potentially irreplaceable, in a time when chaos reigned—and that is a heady feeling. (Courtesy of the Black Hills National Forest Historical Collection, Leland D. Case Library for Western Historical Studies, Black Hills State University.)

The lower levels of Bennett-Clarkson Hospital were evacuated immediately, especially because the location of the hospital was right on Rapid Creek. Here, one can see a corpsman wearing boots, a hard hat, and work clothes to deal with the mud. Truly, mud and silt continued to be mopped and swept up for months after the flooding occurred. (Courtesy of the Black Hills National Forest Historical Collection, Leland D. Case Library for Western Historical Studies, Black Hills State University.)

This image gives a great scale of how high the water got in Bennett-Clarkson Hospital. The man in the image is shoveling the mud and silt out of one of the hallways of the hospital, a necessary job. What makes this image unique, and reiterates the hellish experience the flood was, is the mud on the walls. Visible on the right side of the image, these deposits of mud were not placed on the walls by a human. More likely, these deposits were left after the floodwaters ebbed, leaving a tangible reminder of how deep the water was. It is also likely that the floodwaters did damage to the ceiling of these hallways in the hospital, reiterating the importance of this man's hard hat. Additional damage and previously unfound damage to buildings was found long after floodwaters receded. Even with the recovery process moving quickly, the actual act of recovery took much longer and was much more intricate. (Courtesy of the Black Hills National Forest Historical Collection, Leland D. Case Library for Western Historical Studies, Black Hills State University.)

BIBLIOGRAPHY

Christianson, Corey. "The 1972 Black Hills Flood and the Remaking of Rapid City." *South Dakota History* (Winter 2022): 331–352.

"50th Flood and Greenway Commemoration." City of Rapid City. rapidcityflood.com

"Flood of 1972." Rapid City Public Library. 1972flood.omeka.net

Hennies, Thomas L. *Investigation Report* (Rapid City, SD: Rapid City Police Department, 1972).

"Lessons Learned from Dam Incidents and Failures." Association of State Dam Safety Officials. damfailures.org

Redpath, Bruce B. *Demolition of Ft. Meade Dam, Sturgis, South Dakota, June 1972.* Livermore, CA: US Army Engineer Waterways Experiment Station, Explosive Excavation Research Laboratory, 1973.

South Dakota State Civil Defense Office. *After Action Report on the Black Hills Flood Disaster of June 9–10, 1972.* Pierre, SD: State of South Dakota, 1972.

US Department of Commerce, National Oceanic and Atmospheric Administration (NOAA). *Black Hills Flood of June 9, 1972.* Rockville, MD: Department of Commerce, 1972.

INDEX

DISCOVER THOUSANDS OF LOCAL HISTORY BOOKS FEATURING MILLIONS OF VINTAGE IMAGES

Arcadia Publishing, the leading local history publisher in the United States, is committed to making history accessible and meaningful through publishing books that celebrate and preserve the heritage of America's people and places.

Find more books like this at
www.arcadiapublishing.com

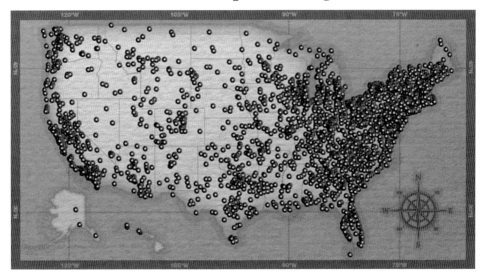

Search for your hometown history, your old stomping grounds, and even your favorite sports team.